Sports Illustrated KIDS

HOCKEY Jokes

by Blake Hoena

illustrated by Daryll Colins

STONE ARCH BOOKS

a capstone imprint

Sports Illustrated Kids All-Star Jokes
is published by Stone Arch Books, a Capstone imprint
1710 Roe Crest Drive
North Mankato, Minnesota 56003
www.mycapstone.com

Cataloging-in-Publication data is available
on the Library of Congress website.

ISBN: 978-1-4965-5090-3 (library binding)
ISBN: 978-1-4965-5094-1 (eBook pdf)

Summary: SPORTS ILLUSTRATED KIDS presents an all-star collection of
HOCKEY jokes, riddles, and memes! With big-shot one-liners like "Why
was the zombie thrown out of the hockey game? There was a face off in the
corner!" these colorful, illustrated joke books will have HOCKEY fans rolling
in the stadium aisles.

Designer: Brann Garvey

Photo Credits:
Sports Illustrated: Damian Strohmeyer, 30, David E. Klutho, 4, 16, 36, 42, 57,
Robert Beck, 26

Printed and bound in Canada.
010382F17

CONTENTS

When you forget
how to hockey...

CHAPTER 1

On the Ice

What animals live at
hockey arenas?

Rink rats.

How do hockey players kiss?

They puck-er up!

Why do hockey players have
numbers on their jerseys?

To remember how many
teeth they've lost.

When do hockey players
dress in formal attire?

When it's a tie game!

How is a hockey player
like a banker?

They both give and
take checks.

Which hockey player has
the biggest skates?

The one with the
biggest feet!

Why was the hockey player
such a bad actor?

She was always
changing her lines.

What do hockey players
and magicians have in common?

Both do hat tricks!

Why are the Swiss bad
hockey players?

They never leave
the neutral zone.

What has twelve feet
and sticks on ice?

A hockey team.

What do you call a pig
that plays hockey?

A puck hog!

What's the difference between
a judge and a skating rink?

One is a justice,
and the other is just ice!

Why did the hockey player
switch to bowling?

He thought it would
be up his alley.

When is a hockey player
like a car?

When he blows a tire.

What kind of hockey skates
wear out quickly?

Cheapskates!

When do hockey players
give each other apples?

Right before scoring
a goal!

How do you know a zombie
is playing ice hockey?

There's a face-off
in the corner!

What's the saddest part
of a hockey rink?

The blue lines.

What do a bad hockey team
and the Titanic have in common?

They both look good
until they hit the ice!

What is the hardest foot
to buy a hockey skate for?

A square foot.

Why was the defender
chewing on the hockey puck?

Because one of the
other players called
it a biscuit!

Two silk worms played a hockey game — who won?

It was a tie!

Two waves played a hockey game — who won?

They tide!

What bug has the best slapshot?

A stick insect!

Why did the hockey player go to jail?

Because he shot the puck.

How did a dog make the
All-Star team?

He was the league's
best stickhandler.

Why did the spotted cat
get disqualified from the
Olympic hockey team?

It was a cheetah!

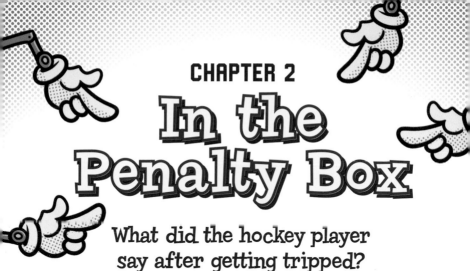

CHAPTER 2
In the Penalty Box

What did the hockey player
say after getting tripped?

That's it — no more
Mr. Ice Guy!

Why did the referee
get a new phone?

Because he's been missing
calls all season.

Why did the player wear swim
trunks in the penalty box?

He got two minutes for diving.

Why did the defender
get arrested?

For trying to kill
the clock.

Why didn't the hockey player
bring his credit cards to the game?

He didn't want to be
penalized for charging.

Why was the defender
holding up an antenna?

She didn't want to get
penalized for causing
interference.

Why did the hockey player
bring an iron to the rink?

He didn't want another
crease violation.

Why did the hockey player ask to go
through airport security again?

He needed to
practice body checks.

Why did the hockey players get
arrested during a power play?

For penalty killing.

What do you call a
cat on the ice?

One cool cat.

Why did the superheroes
meet at the playground?

For a power play!

Why is the pcnatly area
known as a "box"?

Because it's where
people go for fighting.

Why did the hockey player
bring matches to the game?

So she could light
the lamp!

How did the carpenter
end up in the penalty box?

He was penalized
for boarding.

Why did the referee order
the goalie to change his pads?

Because he had five
holes in them.

What's black and white
and never right?

A hockey referee!

What's black and white
and always right?

A zebra with a Ph.D.!

What does a hockey player do
when he loses his eyesight?

Becomes a referee.

Why is a referee like an
angry chicken?

They both have
foul (fowl) mouths.

What kind of tea do hockey
players drink?

Penal-tea!

CHAPTER 3

Goofy Goalies

Which goalkeeper can jump
higher than a crossbar?

All of them — a
crossbar can't jump!

What did the goalie
say to the puck?

"Catch ya later!"

Why was the hockey team's
goalie replaced by a clock?

The clock had
better hands.

What did the grocery store
clerk say to the goalie?

"I've seen coupons that
save more than you!"

Why did the chef steal
the goalie's glove?

Because he needed
a sieve.

Why was the goalie sitting
down and drinking tea?

Because someone put
a biscuit in his basket.

How was the goalie
able to retire early?

He spent all his
time saving.

CHAPTER 4

Fanatic Fans

Why do NHL players
never sweat?

They have too
many fans.

What is another word for
a hockey fan?

A Canadian!

Why was the fan upset?

Because he went to a
boxing match and a hockey
game broke out.

Why did the fans cheer
when a robin flew into the
hockey arena?

They finally got to
see some decent wings.

Why did the hockey rink
suddenly melt?

Because the fans
were heating up.

FAN #1: Bet I can tell you the score
before the game even starts.

FAN #2: Oh yeah, what is it?

FAN #1: 0 - 0

What did the referee do when he
spotted an elephant charging?

He got out of the way!

Why do hockey referees
carry whistles?

In case they get lost
in the action.

FAN #1: Why did our defender
fall down?

FAN #2: He tripped over
the blue line.

Why did the fisherman leave the
hockey game disappointed?

Because it ended
with an empty net.

Why did the fan bring extra
money to the game?

In case she spotted
a yard sale.

CHAPTER 5

What did the coach
give the hockey player who
demanded more money?

A hip check.

Why did the hockey coach
draft a mummy?

Because he had a
nice wrap around!

Why did the coach get frustrated
when he checked his email?

He had too many forwards!

Why did the coach tell his goalie
to bring a tree to the arena?

Because he'd be riding
the pine all game.

Why was the coach so tired?

He was pulling
the goalie.

Why did the coach decide
to draft a honeybee?

She hoped to score a
few buzzer-beaters!

Why was the hockey coach
so full after the game?

His team had too
many turnovers.

What famous hockey player
should have been a coach?

Mike Bossy.

Why did the hockey coach
walk to the game?

Because his wings
were injured.

How do hockey players
celebrate their coach's birthday?

By icing the puck.

Why did the coach visit
the penatly box?

Because his players weren't
answering his texts.

Why did the coach hire a
T. rex to play for him?

They needed more
shorthanded goals.

Hockey player by day...
figure skater by night!

CHAPTER 6

All-Laugh Team

Why do the Boston Bruins disappear
once the hockey season starts?

Because bears hibernate
during the winter.

What penalty are Buffalo Sabers
players often called for?

Slashing!

What NHL team lights
the most lamps?

The Flames!

What do Coyotes and
Panthers have in common?

Neither of them can skate!

Why are the Anaheim Ducks
always so tired?

They wake up at
the quack of dawn.

What do you call a
Penguin helmet?

An ice cap!

How many Wild players
does it take to win the
Stanley Cup?

Nobody knows.

What do you call a Blue Jackets player walking around with the Stanley Cup?

Thief!

How do you keep a Maple Leafs
player out of your yard?

Set up a net.

What's the difference between the
Canucks and the Canadiens?

About twenty
Stanley Cups!

Why did the Toronto coach
fire all of his players?

He was turning over
a new Maple Leaf.

Why don't Columbus fans ever
get cold at the arena?

Because they have
the Blue Jackets.

Why is the ice at
Rogers Place so slippery?

It's the home
of the Oilers.

Why did the Jets' player join
Philidelphia's hockey team?

Because they needed a Flyer.

Knock, knock.
Who's there?
The Jets.
Jets who?
Jets another hockey team that
hasn't won a Stanley Cup.

Why did the New York
fans all go home sick?

They had Islanders fever.

Where do Avalanche players
keep all their money?

In a snowbank.

Why are St. Louis
hockey fans so sad?

Because they've
got the Blues!

What NHL team did the prince
hope to play for one day?

The Los Angeles Kings.

What team always has the
cleanest uniforms?

New Jersey!

Knock, Knock.
Who's there?
Wayne Gretzky!
Wayne who?
Wanye, Wanye, go away. Come again
some other day.

What famous hockey player never
cleaned up after himself?

Mark Messier.

What All-Star hockey player
do cats like the most?

Mario Le-Meow!

Why do the Florida Panthers
drink from bowls?

Because they don't
have any cups!

Which hockey player tells
the best jokes?

Ryan Getzlaf.

And which hockey player thought
all of his jokes were funny?

Guy Lafleur.

What did one Arizona Coyote
say to the other?

Howl's it going?

Knock, Knock.
Who's there?
Carey Price!
Carey who?
Please, Carey my hockey
equipment for me!

Knock, Knock.
Who's there?
Brent Burns!
Brent who?
I think I Brent my hockey stick.

Why should the Nashville Predators
change their name to the Frogs?

They'd be more at
home on the pond!

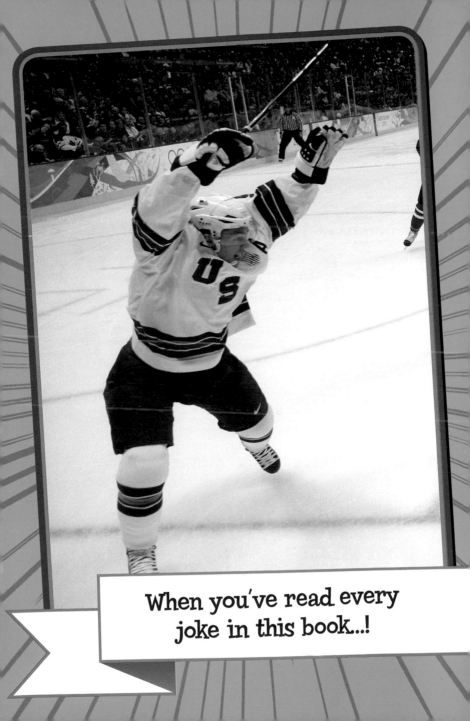

When you've read every
joke in this book...!

How to Tell Jokes

1. KNOW the joke.

Make sure you remember the whole joke before you tell it. This sounds like a no-brainer, but most of us have known someone who says, "Oh, this is so funny . . ." Then, when they tell the joke, they can't remember the end. And that's the whole point of a joke — its punch line.

2. SPEAK CLEARLY.

Don't mumble; don't speak too fast or too slow. Just speak like you normally do. You don't have to use a different voice or accent or sound like someone else. (UNLESS that's part of the joke!)

3. LOOK at your audience.

Good eye contact with your listeners will grab their attention.

4. DON'T WORRY about gestures or how to stand or sit when you tell your joke. Remember, telling a joke is basically talking.

5. DON'T LAUGH at your own joke.

Yeah, yeah, I know some comedians break up while they're acting in a sketch or telling a story, but the best rule to follow is not to laugh. If you start to laugh, you might lose the rhythm of your joke or keep yourself from telling the joke clearly. Let your audience laugh. That's their job. Your job is to be the funny one.

6. THE PUNCH LINE is the most important part of the joke.

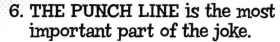

It's the climax, the payoff, the main event. A good joke can sound even better if you pause for just a second or two before you deliver the punch line. That tiny pause will make your audience mentally sit up and hold their breath, eager to hear what's coming next.

7. The SETUP is the second most important part of a joke.

That's basically everything you say before you get to the punch line. And that's why you need to be as clear as you can (see 2 above) so that when you finally reach the punch line, it makes sense!

8. YOU CAN GET FUNNIER.

It's easy. Watch other comedians. Listen to other people tell a joke or story. Check out a good comedy show or film. You can pick up some skills simply by seeing how others get their comedy across. You will absorb it! And soon it will come naturally.

9. Last, but not least, telling a joke is all about TIMING.

That means not only getting the biggest impact for your joke, waiting for the right time, giving that extra pause before the punch line — but it also means knowing when NOT to tell a joke. When you're among friends, you can tell when they'd like to hear something funny. But in an unfamiliar setting, get a "sense of the room" first. Are people having a good time? Or is it a more serious event? A joke has the most funny power when it's told in the right setting.

BLAKE HOENA

Blake Hoena grew up in central Wisconsin. In his youth, he wrote stories about robots conquering the moon and trolls lumbering around the woods behind his parents' house. He now lives in St. Paul, Minnesota, with his wife, two kids, a dog, and a couple of cats. Blake continues to make up stories about things like space aliens and superheroes, and he has written more than 70 chapter books, graphic novels, and joke books for children.

DARYLL COLLINS

Daryll Collins is a professional illustrator in the areas of magazine & newspaper illustration, children's books, character design & development, advertising, comic strips, greeting cards, games, and more! His clients range from Sports Illustrated Kids and Boys' Life magazine to McDonald's and the US Postal Service. He currently lives in Kentucky.

Joke Dictionary!

bit (BIT)—a section of a comedy routine

comedian (kuh-MEE-dee-uhn)—an entertainer who makes people laugh

headliner (HED-lye-ner)—the last comedian to perform in a show

improvisation (im-PRAH-vuh-ZAY-shuhn)—a performance that hasn't been planned; "improv" for short

lineup (LINE-uhp)—a list of people who are going to perform in a show

one-liner (WUHN-lye-ner)—a short joke or funny remark

open mike (OH-puhn MIKE)—an event at which anyone can use the microphone to perform for the audience

punch line (PUHNCH line)—the words at the end of a joke that make it funny or surprising

shtick (SHTIK)—a repetitive, comic performance or routine

segue (SEG-way)—a sentence or phrase that leads from one joke or routine to another

stand-up (STAND-uhp)—a stand-up comedian performs while standing alone on stage

timing (TIME-ing)—the use of rhythm and tempo to make the joke funnier

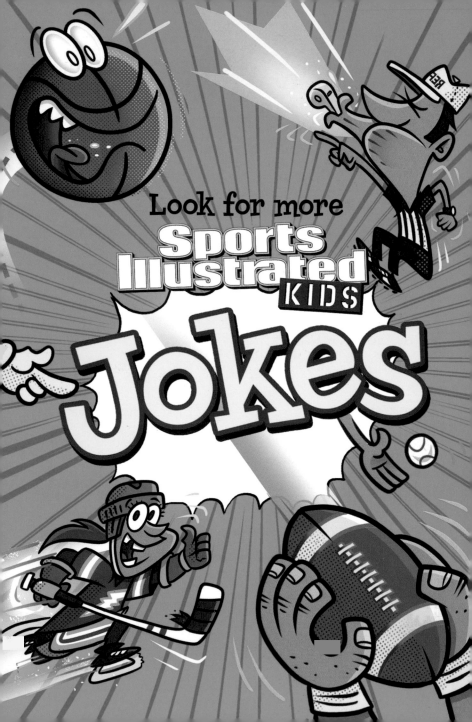

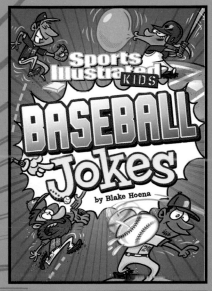

Sports Illustrated KIDS

BASEBALL Jokes

by Blake Hoena

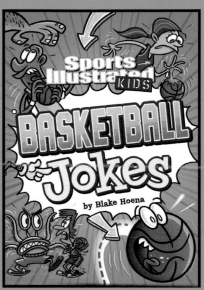

Sports Illustrated KIDS

BASKETBALL Jokes

by Blake Hoena

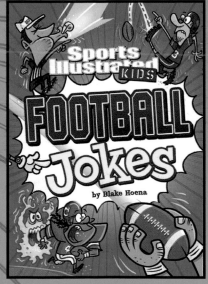

Sports Illustrated KIDS

FOOTBALL Jokes

by Blake Hoena

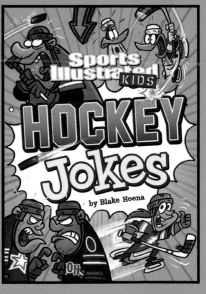

Sports Illustrated KIDS

HOCKEY Jokes

by Blake Hoena

FACTHOUND

Use FactHound to find Internet sites related to this book.

Visit www.facthound.com

Just type in 9781496550903 and go.

 Check out projects, games and lots more at
www.capstonekids.com